Looking for Georgia O'Keeffe
and other
OBSERVATIONS

for Marilyn ——

Ri Weester
12/31/89

By the same author

A THIN BODY OF WORK
SUNFLOWERS
LET IT BE A DANCE
HIS & HERS
DRAGONFLIES, CODFISH & FROGS
(formerly Speaking Poems)
THE VOICE OF THE HIVE
STARK NAKED
EVEN AS WE SPEAK
DESERTED ROOSTER
THEY ARE ALL GONE NOW
NOTICE ME!

LOOKING
for Georgia O'Keeffe
and other
OBSERVATIONS

by
Ric Masten

Artwork by Reed Farrington

SUNFLOWER INK
3 Palo Colorado Road
Carmel, California 93923

ACKNOWLEDGMENTS:

Thanks to Embree, for catching my mistakes and for being as close to us as seven lengths of hose.

Thanks to Tom Owen-Towle, who never fails to find typos but always after the book has been printed. This time, however, consenting to do a proof-read before publication so any errors that slip through are Ton's fault.

Thanks to Kris and Celeste of Instant Type for daring to keep the doors open.

Library of Congress Catalogue Card No. 87-062633

ISBN 0-931104-22-X

For Nathan, Taylor, Ricky & Cara

Contents

**RAISING HOGS
FOR FUN AND PROFIT** 51

**HAPPY ENDINGS
IN THE BADLANDS** 77

Georgia O'Keeffe

Author's Note

Invited to do some readings at a conference held at Ghost Ranch, New Mexico, I was delighted at the unexpected windfall: at long last an all-expense-paid opportunity to visit Georgia O'Keeffe country, and put myself in close proximity to an artist whose lifework had become so important to me. Not that I would have looked her up. Word had it that the old woman could be quite curt with intrusive fans, having slammed the door in more than one pilgrim's face. However, shortly before the time came for my trip to the high desert, at ninety-nine, Georgia O'Keeffe passed away. I could only hope that her after-glow had not faded completely from the landscape she had made so familiar to me.

Sharing these thoughts with the conference audience, I also mentioned how disappointed I was to discover her beloved residence in Abiquiu had been transformed into a kind of museum. Copies of her canvases miniaturized down to post-card size and then peddled to tourists who were really looking for pictures of Indians. Browsing around, I had the distinct feeling that T-shirts and ash trays were already in the works.

At lunch the next day, a man at my table introduced himself as an artist and also a fellow Georgia O'Keeffe enthusiast. Then leaning close, like someone with a secret to tell, he whispered, "Would you like to visit the adobe she spent her last years in? It's quite close by." He went on to tell me that he had found her place that very morning and was still trembling from the experience. "Her slippers," he said, "looked as if she had just stepped out of them."

That evening, the poem **Looking for Georgia O'Keeffe** was born. Later, while searching for a poem to lead off and set the tone for this collection, I realized that the kind of things I had been writing about recently, were the same things I went looking for out at Georgia O'Keeffe's that late summer afternoon.

Her courage as a creative person was remarkable. Inflexible when it came to her vision, she was able to show us the world as she saw it, detached from the vogue and vagaries of the changing art scene. Using her wonderfully wry wit, she shrugged off critics like so many deerflies. The Native Americans have a saying that catches the essence of such people: "He arose each morning and braided his hair because he knew he was an arrow-maker."

And then there is this business of aging, of growing old gracefully. Nearly sixty myself, someone like Georgia O'Keeffe shines like a beacon of encouragement for youngsters my age. In her nineties she took up potting with teenage enthusiasm, and when the clay would not do what she wanted it to, undaunted, she said simply, "I must press on." The reader will find much "pressing on" between the covers of this book.

But most of all I am taken by her humanness. Here we have an artist whose work was widely acclaimed in her own lifetime, a tall dark graceful beauty, documented in a series of striking photographs taken by her husband Alfred Stieglitz; and yet when asked about reincarnation, her biographer reports that she wanted to come back as a petite blond with a beautiful soprano voice. "I would sing," she said, "very high, very clear notes. Without fear."

And my not knowing whether to laugh or cry at this candid remark is really what most of the observations that follow are all about.

Ric Masten
Carmel, California

Looking
for Georgia O'Keeffe

LOOKING
FOR GEORGIA O'KEEFFE

there are stories...horror stories!
and if the old woman were still alive
i would never have made the pilgrimage
to her Ghost Ranch residence

Bill Sozi
says she was anything but menacing
of course he is Native American
and a lunatic to boot
a painter of abstract buffalo
who thinks his head is on fire
and in the Southwest
no one pays attention to an artist
who isn't Gorman slick
or DiGratzi cute

no one
except perhaps Georgia O'Keeffe
at least
that's what i chose to believe
as i circled her remote adobe
a sneak thief window-peeking
stealing looks
through cracks in the blinds
a pair of red slippers—
the glimpse of an empty easel—
shadows on a stripped bed
and out back a ramada
black as a Penitente cross
against a sheet of high twilight sky
the enclosed garden overgrown
hollyhocks
broken down and gone to seed

brown patio walls hung
with the bleached bones
she had so lovingly rendered
and the view
i took that in too
filling my eyes
with the distant line of the Pedernal
floating above a sculpture
of salmon-colored hills

all the while
afraid that someone would come
and catch me making off
with this priceless ambience
Juan Hamilton
her protegé and beneficiary
arriving in a rage
to collar the robber—call the police

hurriedly
i picked a twig of sage
a remembrance
from the hem of the rutted driveway
and ran back to the car
        back to the coast
where everything is close
to Silicon Valley
and a hard copy
of an emotional experience
resembles the high country
about as much as a picture postcard
sent from Abiquiu, New Mexico

THE VALUE OF TAXIDERMY

an egocentric
displays his medals
and knows the value of taxidermy
others claim that they can catch
a record-setting trout
and then release it
without showing it off

stuffed and mounted
some fish stories
do not appear at all
lifelike

but when we stop talking religion
we discover
both of us know
that the other side of the pillow
is the cool side
both of us sit
in public restrooms
stooled
and staring at the tile floor
making patterns with our eyes

fished
from an examined life
i present the trophies—
proof positive
that even the lonely
are not alone
alone

i despise every minute
i must put in
with a whip and a chair

THE LION TAMER
ENTERS THE THESAURUS
AND ESCAPES WITH HIS LIFE

i don't like to write!

words are nasty
uncooperative animals
stubborn unruly beasts
and i despise every minute
i must put in
with a whip and a chair
trying to make them behave

sure i take a bow
when i have them
all lined up in an impressive row
my vulnerable ego
having somehow escaped
critical analysis without
being clawed or bitten
but i don't like to write

i like having written

THE PLIGHT
OF THE SERIOUS WRITER

i once complained
to an astute and insightful
writer friend of mine
about being bogged down
in a torturously long
and nonproductive dry spell

gravely
he considered my sad situation
then
with great compassion
and empathy
said:

"so life
  is treating you that well
  is it?"

A CRASH COURSE
IN AMERICAN

the study
and composition of poetry
does not always occur
in the English Department
you know

for instance in Japan
at the University of Tokyo
the poets are all
in the Japanese Department

THE JUMP START

"remember Clyde?
from high school?
tall gangly kid—
thick horn-rim glasses—
ol' coke-bottle eyes
sat behind Sue Douglas in calculus
always goosing her with his slide-rule
that Clyde — remember him?
you do?
well
did you know he died?"

in this way
established writers
and other creative old-timers
prime the engine on cold mornings

dropping by for a cup of tea
the murder mystery writer
flops down on a kitchen chair
announcing
that Kate Smith just passed away
to which
a poet's only response can be—
"i wonder who's next
they go in groups of three
you know"

at other times
when there's nothing worth noting
in the obits
they simply sit together
comparing
suspicious-looking moles

having a great old time
talking tumors

until
with eyes suddenly alive
the novelist jumps up
and whistling something
from an old Walt Disney movie
dashes off
to hack and slash his way
through another chapter
of literary mayhem

the poet
kindled
with new found enthusiasm
once again able
to delight the world
with more depressing fare
about death divorce suicide
and despair

FOR A PUBLIC SPEAKER
IS THERE LIFE AFTER DEATH?
for Virginia Rose

"...but Doctor
how could you possibly
have removed the wrong leg?"
i suppose
worse mistakes have been made—

nevertheless
mine was the kind of nightmare
one would give absolutely anything
to go to sleep from
and as you know Virginia
i wasn't there
so i can only surmise
what the program chair feels
fifteen minutes into the vacuum
and four hundred eyes on the door

somewhat akin i expect
to the panic that paralyzed my end
when putting the receiver to my ear
i heard your icy voice inquire
"why aren't you here?"

one thing i do know for sure
beyond excruciating and unbearable
levels of pain and shame
are indistinguishable

looking for ways to make amends
i have considered sending you
my life savings—
my first born child—
looking for absolution
i have called everyone i know
everyone except you Virginia

you i could only face
through the mail
and i do hope
you took some satisfaction
from the detailed suicide note

as for the larger picture—
in the world news that very evening
it was reported that astronomers
in Australia
watched a star explode—
an extremely rare phenomenon
which
traveling at the speed of light
happened 150 million years ago

the prediction is
that the noticeable aftermath
left by this distant apocalypse
will dominate the night sky
down under
for centuries to come

and i do lie awake Virginia
wondering
just what exactly
has been cut off here
at the knee

your mildewed remains

CLOSET POET

for Michael Forrest

i suspect you know precisely
how many poems fit in a cardboard box
perhaps even
the number of boxes it takes
before the furniture must go

who are you keeping
these secrets for though?
yourself?
and/or that vague romantic
notion you have
of being found in a musty attic
some future kindred spirit
sitting on a dusty trunk
weeping
over your mildewed remains

Emily Dickinson
was already at the cemetery
when Colonel Tom Higginson
went to the closet
and discovered her collection of damask
hand-sewn dreams
neatly folded away like fine linen

lucky for us
he and her inheritors
were a determined
self-serving enterprising bunch

certainly everyone admires
a shy private person
but be advised

without the pump of ambition
all the talent in the world
can come to no more than a couple of trips
to the dump

UNIMPRESSED

i offered to drive him
to the theater
hoping that he could tell
by my actions
that i was not one
to be overwhelmed
by important people

with this established
and i might add
understood
i slipped behind the wheel
turned on the windshield wiper
and unlatched the hood

no-sir-ee!
no autographs for me

TALKIN' ON THE TALK SHOW
for Gary Tessler, KOA Denver

every Friday at 11:45 Denver time
i, as a "regular feature of the show"
drop everything
and expose myself to millions
—an electronic flasher

lowering my voice
i try to project Orson Wells
reciting the Old Testament
but secretly suspect
it sounds more like Mickey Mouse
with nothing to say—hi kids!

and how can i be certain
i'm not just standing in a closet
hearing voices—talking to myself

a hundred years ago
if i'd been caught doing this
they'd have put me away for sure
the orderlies exchanging glances
as i desperately try to explain
about having a Talk Show Host in my ear

nevertheless
every Friday at 11:45 Denver time
i duck into a telephone booth
and like Clark Kent
pray that this morning
i remembered
to put on clean leotards

my God!
it's all so religious
this casting bread upon the airwaves

and a true believer never doubts
the existence of a listening audience

he simply says his prayers
hangs up
and goes on about his business

The Day
of the Dogfish

THE DAY OF THE DOGFISH

July 1970
the night of the salmon bake
Tank Richards nearly O.D.'d
after which
the entire youth group
confessed to using dope
and was summarily expelled from the grounds
the older generation left behind
to wrestle with hypocrisy
"happy hour" in ruins
but then a successful conference
always needs
some real crisis to deal with
as Black Elk says
"where the path of difficulty
 crosses the easy way
 mark a holy place"

seventeen summers later
the incident
that would galvanize
the camp community appeared
almost laughable by comparison
it seems
some of the seventh grade boys
had cornered and killed
a dogfish
at the shallow end of the lagoon
and then
chased the girls around
waving the carcass overhead

well—
you might have thought
civilization had collapsed then and there

the Dean instantly scheduling
an emergency meeting
to precede the evening's activities
(which
as fate would have it
was a memorial service
commemorating the anniversary
of the bombing of Hiroshima)

all campers will attend!
no one is excused!
and i as theme speaker
was chosen to try and put
the day of the dogfish to rest

to ask out loud
if what started out innocently enough—
a young fisherman
attempting to remove Jaws
(dogfish are small sharks)
from the swimming area
turning into a killing frenzy?
one eyewitness said
he saw boys with sticks
stabbing and clubbing
till the water ran red
or was it
as others would insist
a rush to be humane?
to put a mortally wounded creature
out of its misery and pain

an act of kindness?
an act of brutality?
like *Rashomon*

24

everyone saw
what they wanted to see

as for me
i remembered
the birthday boy
with his brand-new pellet gun
and the skunk
that began as a target—
a tin can—
but when hit transformed itself
into a living breathing thing
hurt and suffering
my weapon not powerful enough
for a clean kill
i shot and shot and shot
sickened and horrified
at the kaleidoscope of expression
in the dying animal's eyes
it was the death lesson
that haunts me still

as for the accusation
that using the fish
to tease the girls
showed somehow
that these young men
had little respect for life
prompted me to tell the story
about the time my own kids
were willing to die
trying to save Ol' Strut & Cluck
from the frying pan
Pocahontas throwing herself
across the chopping block

25

then
even before the severed head
had hit the ground
triumphantly marching
the bloody squirming body around

my God!
it's the *Lord of the Flies*
i thought
until someone older and wiser
suggested that children
can make the transition
between something living
and something dead
more quickly than adults can

this event
these memories
dredging up the song i sang
decades ago
at anti-war demonstrations
a song that concluded

" You can multiply the lemming
  Till they rush into the sea.
  But what have suicidal rodents
  Got to do with you and me?
  We might have split the atom
  But to worry is absurd,
  And yet
  My son is in the garden
  Trying to kill a bird."

and recalling this
i also recalled

that once in a Unitarian church
a gang of angry women
demanded that i explain
my metaphor
and when they learned
that i had given my son
a BB gun for Christmas
they were upon me like barracuda
ripping and tearing
but just when it looked like
i was a goner for sure
a young stranger jumped in
and hauled me out with this

"i was raised a Quaker"
he said
"forbidden even to have a friend
  who owned a gun
  and so
  in my rebellious years
  i declared my independence
  by joining the Marines
  and oh how i wish now
  i could have learned about death
  from a skunk a bird or a fish
  you see
  the first thing i killed
  was human"

and that was the end of that
and this too
the camp community
filing out of the meeting house
and down to the lagoon
where we launched

our fleet of *toro*
floating paper lanterns
each one lit with a candle
to represent the soul
of a human being
who perished at Hiroshima

there on the shore we stood
singing hymns
clinging to each other
till time
extinguished every light
and in darkness we vanished
leaving the dogfish
to move instinctively
through their watery night

> *the Eliot Institute*
> *Seabeck, Washington*
> *Summer Conference 1987*

PINKY RANG THE BELL!

(Song lyric)

We stepped upon the stage of life.
Now, let me set the scene.
The players came from miles around
And gathered on the green.
Parts were given, lines were learned,
The show was going well.
It looked like it would be a hit
'Till Pinky rang the bell.

Pinky rang the bell!
Pinky rang the bell!
It looked like it would be a hit
'Till Pinky rang the bell.

The teacher came with thoughts to think,
The poet, words to feel.
The lawyer had the law to keep,
The nurse had hurts to heal.
The soldier brought a gun to shoot,
The salesman things to sell.
But we never got it off the ground,
'Cause Pinky rang the bell.

Pinky rang the bell!
Pinky rang the bell!
We never got it off the ground
'Cause Pinky rang the bell.

He said he'd seen the play before
And knew how it would end.
"The tragedy repeats itself
  Time and time again."
The actors and the audience
Get caught up in its spell.
And we would have played the drama out
But Pinky rang the bell.

29

Pinky rang the bell!
Pinky rang the bell!
We would have played the drama out
But Pinky rang the bell.

And then there came the theater fire
And how the flames did rage.
Romeo and Juliet
Could not get off the stage.
And there we were, the bunch of us,
On our way to hell.
You and I threw up our hands
But Pinky rang the bell.

Pinky rang the bell!
Pinky rang the bell!
You and I threw up our hands
But Pinky rang the bell.

And now I sit upon my bed
Clipping the reviews.
I played my part as best I could,
Picking up the cues.
Don't ask me what his motives were
For who can truly tell?
The question is just where were you
When Pinky rang the bell?

the Eliot Institute
Seabeck, Washington
Summer Conference 1970

A SPECTATOR SPORT

pretending
to be vitally interested
in road racing
i tune in
the Iran-Contra hearings
a spectacle
not unlike the Indianapolis 500
appealing
to the side of my nature
that cranes its neck
secretly
hoping to see
a fatal accident

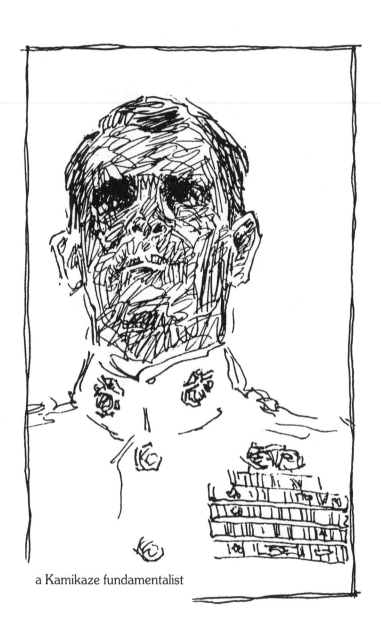

a Kamikaze fundamentalist

THE DIVINE WIND

human nature being what it is—
the military arsenal
being what it has become—
questions arise

backed
into the same desperate corner
would a Napoleonic paper-hanger
commit suicide these days?
or apocalypse?

pushed to the brink
do you think a godless dirty-Commie
would surrender unconditionally
to a Capitalist pig?
or vice versa?

the fact is an atheist
might be less inclined
to blow up the here and now
than those among us who believe
in a sweet by-and-by

there is no defense
against a Kamikaze fundamentalist
willing to die flying prophecy
down the smokestack of human existence

even so
the heavy-weights pose and bristle
confident as battleships
while dissidents on both sides
are ordered to get their thinking straight

MONKEY BUSINESS

aside from the cover
of *National Sleaze* magazine
it was the last time
the candidate in question
was publicly seen (wrong!)

but just suppose
the attractive long-legged
"friend of a friend"
had turned out to be a brilliant
young political scientist
top of her class
trained in more than biology
only there to advise
and explain her Ph.D. thesis
on winning Presidential campaigns

sure!
and there really is a tooth fairy!
the man in the street
would wink and exclaim

reaffirming an attitude
that people under thirty
should be polishing the brass
that beautiful people
are not too fast in the head
and if it's a woman
then
get your sweet ass back in bed

ANATOMY OF A ZEALOT

"machines
have been devised
to accurately measure
the age of found objects
so what we have here
has got to be
the remains of Noah's Ark
never mind
the bones of dinosaurs
they were cleverly put here
to test our faith"

in matters religious
one reaches the truth
only
through good hard
investigative thought
however when one
is thoroughly convinced
that the truth is found
it then
becomes necessary
to stop thinking

THE SECOND COMING

go!
tell the Catholics
tell the Protestants
the Millennium is here!
at long last
God has acknowledged
two thousand years
of prayers prayed

Jesus has reappeared
in all his glory!

i know
because i saw him
at the Hospice
tenderly washing the feet
of a man who was dying
of AIDs

WHAT HATH
THE SURGEON GENERAL WROUGHT?

i gave smoking up years ago
but simply
couldn't bring myself
to throw away my favorite pipe—
my charred old briar pot

and sometimes
over coffee
or when i'm at the typewriter
between thoughts
or on the telephone
waiting to be connected
the compulsion to light up
lingers
like the smell of Rum & Maple
in the living room drapes

but everywhere i go
these days
the Gestapo
watches every move i make

rounding an undulating corner
i half expect to see Indiana Jones

THE PRESS
AND THE PRESIDENTIAL POLYP

suddenly the mind of America
focuses
on the place where the sun never shines

like characters
in a George Lukas movie
we are hurtled
down a mile of twisting colon
light from the flexible sigmoidoscope
probing ahead
till rounding an undulating corner
i half expect to see Indiana Jones
leaning against an abnormal outcropping
a devil-may-care smile on his face

all the time Dan Rather
like a Greyline tour guide
calling out points of interest
carefully explaining that the bowels
in which we were trespassing
were not actually the President's
talk about an invasion
of someone's privacy!

of course
for the delighted proctologist
it was all money in the bank
but for those of us who blanch
at the thought of a rubber glove
afraid to chance a medical check-up
for fear of what the doctor might find
believe me
these have been difficult times

i mean if the Commander in Chief's
villous adenoma can go undetected
what hope do the rank and file have?

it would seem then
that an unrestrained press
has once again
left the American public
en masse
with a quizzical finger
up its collective—

PORTRAIT OF A MOTHER
WAITING FOR THE OTHER
SHOE TO FALL

what's a mother to do
when a son
with no visible means of support
wears Salvador Ferragamos
drives a Maserati
and makes payments
on a two-thousand-dollar-a-month apartment

what else
but wonder out loud
about the enormous diamond ring
even Liberace
would have found tasteless

"don't worry Mom
  it costs a lot less
  than you'd think"

and for the life of me
she mused
laughing darkly
i can't decide
whether that was the good
or the bad news

HE BEING HEFTY
AND SHE FULL-FIGURED

Don Rickles' sense of humor
would seem mean and vicious
coming out of Robert Redford
so
i hope i'm bald enough
and funny enough looking
in a bathing suit
to get away
with telling you about
what came to mind
during the tender performance
of a love song
composed and rendered
by a fat man
for his even fatter fiance

a seaside song
a two silhouettes
walking the silver strand
hand in hand type song
windswept
with salty kisses
and ocean spray
a beautiful day in a love-
life song
but
when you know
you're not supposed to think
about whales
whales
are all you can think about

beached whales
frolicking in the surf

the scene
in *From Here To Eternity*
played out
on an immense corpulent scale
tons of fun heaped
on a wet slippery rock
collapsing the dock
acres and acres of sunburn
and footprints two-feet deep

caught
in the undertow
swept along on a riptide
of uncontrollable thought
i almost miss
what is most important here
set to music—in song
all of us appear
ageless attractive and trim
able to see each other
as he saw her and she saw him

last seen
climbing higher in the sad green trees

THE ORANGUTANS

on public television
there were pictures of a Canadian woman
a devoted naturalist
living in the rain forest of Sumatra

her husband
formerly her tracker
and a native of the region
was described
as having an uncanny ability
to locate wild orangutans
another woman
might have settled for
a captain of industry

aside from the comic relief
however
this well-intentioned documentary
was for the most part
standard
Beauty and the Beast

at least
for those of us who have been
to the Philadelphia zoo
and seen the caged gorilla
with such melancholy
etched into his giant face
we all wept openly
and this
certainly looked
like more of the same

which it was
ending with our heroine

standing beneath the jungle canopy
looking up
trying to extend our apologies

the golden primates
last seen
climbing higher in the sad green trees
slowly pulling themselves up
hand over hand

MAGIC MOUNTAIN
(Song lyric)

Little children run
Behind a military band.
Precious seeds are buried
In some godforsaken land.
And the pacifist ain't got
No fingers on his hand.
But up on magic mountain
The view is mighty grand.

The tatooed sailor swears,
Cuts the hair off his flower child.
He's got pictures on his abdomen
To make the ladies smile.
And no one bakes a cake
Or sends the prisoners a file.
But up on magic mountain
You can see a hundred miles.

Chocolate-colored Barbie Dolls,
A dollar ninety-eight on sale.
And bottles full of chemicals
To make the body pale.
And picture windows framin'
The neighbor's garbage pail.
But up on magic mountain
The mist hangs like a veil.

And you could miss the sunset
If you're diggin' in a hole.
Or scatter dirt around
Until you cover up your soul.
And there are lots of hungry actors
Ain't ever gonna get a role.
But up on magic mountain
The sky is so clear and cold.

47

Pilgrims come for water
And they pause to dig the view.
They ask about the magic,
'Cause they want to get some too.
So you tell 'em somethin' funny
'Cause you're the old guru.
And the magic on the mountain
Comes up the hill inside of you.

And livin' in a desert
That don't mean that you won't drown.
And the fallen woman, she's the one
You love to be around.
So you listen in the evenin'
'Til you hear her breathin' sound,
And up on magic mountain
You realize it's time to come down.

Yeah,
Up on magic mountain
You realize it's time to come down.

**Raising Hogs
for Fun and Profit**

RAISING HOGS
FOR FUN AND PROFIT

take it from me
if you ever
have anything to do with pigs
you can bet
there will always be
a story in it

this holds true
in urban
as well
as rural settings

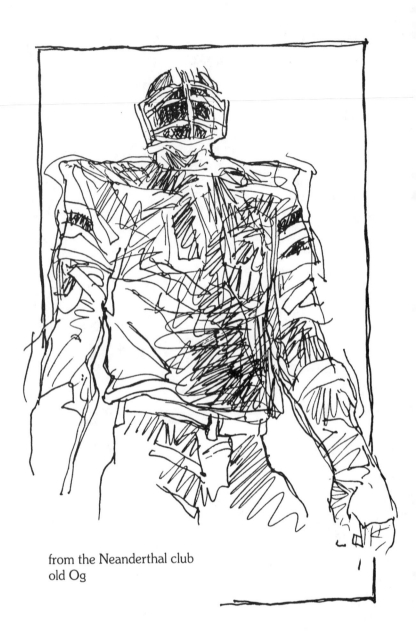

from the Neanderthal club
old Og

FOR SUCH A BRUTAL
PRIMITIVE SPORT
I MUST APOLOGIZE

ladies
i hate to admit it
but there are times when i find
i haven't completely resigned
from the Neanderthal club
old Og
still needs a way to deal
with pent-up aggression
explaining perhaps
why the trip to the Super Bowl
has become such a national
obsession

but then
isn't it more humane and genteel
to tame the beast vicariously?
to sit
harmlessly watching a field
where padded paid professionals
hit and flog each other
isn't this better
than taking it out on the wife
the kids the dog and your mother?
to say nothing
about just possibly reducing
the risk of World War III

ladies i put it to you
isn't football
really
the civilized thing to do?

WIDOWS OF THE NFL

during the season
do not arrange social engagements
unless you have checked
with him first
all dates are in doubt
Sundays are sacred of course
but since Monday-night football
is now played on Thursday
rational thinking is out

and don't
try to circumvent this
by inviting friends over
to watch the game with your spouse
if they root for the other city
then the scene in the den
will not be pretty
and probably end
with a swat team surrounding your house

however
if the cheering section is compatible
do plan to serve snacks
during the action
not hor d'oeuvres
nothing fancy like that
just be sure to include something
from the five major food groups
caffeine alcohol sugar salt
and fat

and don't assume
he's enjoying himself
rabid football fans

are perpetually wretched
touchdowns ahead
they still feel defeated
convinced that they can't keep the lead
down by a point and it's hopeless
"we'll never score what we need!"

and it's really OK
for women to hate the game
better this
than pretending to be a fan
a "sports buddy"
with a bright inquiring mind
trying to impress him
with questions
about nickelbacks and pointspread
while he watches his team
fall a field goal behind

but most of all
after the opening whistle has blown
don't get sexy
studies have shown
football renders the male impotent
at game time cold showers are best
besides if you think about it
you have your own hands-off policy
during *Dynasty*
and *Falcon Crest*

keep in mind though
the road to the Super Bowl
may seem endless

but a frustrated maid must
not lose faith as she
lies alone in her bed
when the Pro Bowl is over
so is the season
and the couch potato
will
rise from the dead

A HUNDRED YARDS OF CLICHES
AND HACKNEYED IDIOMS

GOAL LINE
on any given Sunday
a classic match-up
with play-off implications
and here to cover the action
a man who needs no introduction
before an overflow crowd
the gladiators take the field
in what should be a high-scoring affair
the weather not a factor
the smell of upset in the air
    10
coming forward he meets the ball
the pigskin is rooted a mile
fielded cleanly
a world-class sprinter
scoots up the alley
cuts back against the grain
runs into a brick wall
the zebras unscramble the pile
shaking the cobwebs away
he'll think about that for awhile
    20
barking out the signals
he takes the snap
sees some daylight . . . ka-pow!
the big guy closes the door
it depends on where they spot the ball
the chain gang comes in
too early to gamble
turning it over they boot it away
it's a game of inches
and both teams came to play

30
lost in the sun
coughing it up
digging it out of the dirt
he'll have to eat it right there
they dodged a bullet that time
the field general goes to work
the men in the trenches stay home
earning their keep
it's a physical sport
and nothing comes cheap
40
marching down the field
flags flying
that'll come back to haunt 'em
they come away empty
great protection
relentless pursuit
goose eggs up on the score board
the outcome remains a mystery
the seconds tick away
the first half is history
MIDFIELD
back to the drawing board
conferring with the men upstairs
making the adjustments
changing the game plan
they know they're in a ball game now
rallying the troops
i wonder what he's telling them in there?
the second half holds the answer
and while waiting for play to resume
a word from our sponsor

40
they came right out firing
throwing up the bomb
going for all the marbles
dodging the sack
he scrambles around in the pocket
connecting for a bundle
on a roll
he reaches into his bag of tricks
it's the old Statue of Liberty
chalk up a quick six
30
the extra point goes astray
a kicker's life is a lonely one
mistakes will kill you
fielding the pumpkin he breaks one loose
motoring coast to coast
it's a brand new ballgame now
splitting the uprights they go on top
the momentum swings
but there's lots of time on the clock
it ain't over till the fat lady sings
20
a seesaw battle
an all-out war
the crowd is beside itself
what they need now is a score
an immaculate reception
he goes to the shotgun
they come with the blitz
it goes down to the wire
a Hail Mary at the gun
pulling a squeaker out of the fire

10

you do what you have to do
go with what got you there
it was a barn burner
they simply didn't have the horses
all hands can stand tall
someone wins...someone loses
that's the name of the game
you go out and give it your all
no question about it
that's football
       ENDZONE

(The score: 12 to 7)

SHOPPING FOR CLOTHES
BY GENDER

much
of what makes up my wardrobe
began as a gift
an unpleasant birthday
or Christmas surprise
shirts and ties
i would never have bought
for myself
but in the name of thrift wore
and in wearing
developed a great fondness for
and when such
an article of clothing dies
a man grieves
thereafter standing briefly
in the doorway of habadasheries
eyes sweeping rack and shelf
and if nothing there
looks familiar
leaves
before the clerk can say
"may i be of help?"

in this way i can do
an entire shopping center
in about the time it takes
to walk through it

on the flip side of this
my wife
picks out everything she wears
but wears nothing out
too fickle for that
her relationship with apparel
is more of a fling

61

a short-lived affair
good for a couple of dates
then snubbed and dismissed
as "that old thing"

entering a boutique
the woman is always on the make
unwilling to leave
until she has danced
with every rag on the rack
taken them all for a spin
in the mirror
a patrotic fashion plate
she seems determined
to spend eternity on parade
wrapping
herself in flags
put on hold
aimlessly wandering the mall
i stop at the window display
of a cutlery shop
and while counting the blades
on a Swiss Army knife
come up with an axiom
sharp enough
to almost hold true

> when
> shopping for clothes
> men
> look for old friends
> women for new

A DIET
TO END ALL DIETS

for some people
and i happen to be one
there is no such thing
as a successful diet
the only way i can lose weight
is to stop eating completely
and start to die

then just this side of death
start eating again
and for a couple of weeks
or at least
until i'm taken off
the critical list
i look great!

GASTRONOMICS

sometimes...
after a thankless job
when the "Ricky's been a good boy"
feelings abound
i like to take a friend out to dinner
at the best restaurant in town
the classy one where the walls
are made of mirrors
and the maitre d' hovers
like the prince of darkness

in the lounge
waiting for a table to vacate
i anticipate the feast
what will it be
lobster thermidor or chateaubriand?
an appetizer of course
blue points on the half shell
flown in daily from the East
artichoke soup
Caesar salad
and later over an aperitif
i'll have the baked Alaska
or chocolate mousse

"go for it!" i tell myself
"and damn the expense!"

pad and pencil poised
the waiter waits
as i study
the selection of epicurean joys
a culinary Don Juan
unable to make a commitment

that is until my dinner guest
announces
that he is picking up the tab
overriding my objection
with "no no i insist!"

a pronouncement
that sends my attention
scrambling sideways like a crab
to the price list on the right

"the vegetable plate sounds nice"
says i
waving goodbye to my appetite

"and for dessert
 i'll try the bread pudding"

THE DINNER SONG
(Song lyric)

I been runnin' a rat race
'Round and around.
Makin' up songs
At a dollar a pound.
Crankin' out music.
Thinkin' up rhymes.
Pourin' my heart out
for nickels and dimes.
>   But the song that I bring ya,
>   The song that I sing ya
>   It ain't the saleable kind.
>   It's just the song, I bring along
>   To give ya,
>   When I come to dinner.

We've done up the dishes.
Got 'em stacked away.
Then someone inquires
Whether I'd like to play.
Well, I thought you'd never ask me.
I believe that's my line
As I take out my axe
And you break out the wine.
>   And the song that I bring ya,
>   The song that I sing ya
>   It was wrote for just such a time.
>   It's just the song, I bring along
>   To give ya,
>   When I come to dinner.

The room gets all quiet
As I softly begin.
Then right about here
The baby crawls in.

The dog gets to barkin',
The telephone rings.
And all hell breaks loose
When I start to sing.
>The song that I bring ya,
>That I'm tryin' to sing ya
>But ya don't have to hear
>The whole thing...

>It's just the song, I bring along
>To give ya,
>When I come to dinner.

Well, it's been a good evenin'.
I've had a fun time.
And I'd like to leave
A little something behind.
So that maybe tomorrow
After I'm gone
Y'all find you're still hummin'
On a piece of my song.
>And that's why I sung it.
>That's why I brung it.
>That's why I gave it
>Loud and strong.
>I sing my song
>So that maybe later on,
>Y'all think of me...
>And ask me back to dinner.

a bird in the mailbox
peeking out

ADVENTURES
IN THE NASAL PASSAGE

at even
the slightest suggestion
of a bird in the mailbox
peeking out
interpersonal communication
takes a real nose dive

faced with this distracting
situation
victory over death
a sure-fire get-rich-quick plan
erotic dissertations on sex
no topic
can override my desire
to conjure up a box of Kleenex—
a handkerchief—
a shirtcuff for God's sake!

where are the public relations
people when we need them?

if this much-maligned object
could somehow be imbued
with an air of glamor
a sighting might become
a positive experience
not something
to turn away from in disgust

this having been accomplished
no doubt
societies would quickly form
and like the Audubon

go on field trips—
every novice
eager to spot a barn owl
"the trick Mildred
  is in knowing where to look"

enthusing like rockhounds
"wow!
  look at the beauty Jack found!"

like wild flowers
the prizes picked
and pressed between the pages
of leather-bound books—
valuable human achievements
not unlike tears

and in recognizing this
we take another tentative step
away from
an incapacitating prejudice—
able
to lunch with Quasimodo
without a second thought

AN EXERCISE IN CARING

remaining close
to a chronic case of halitosis
must certainly
be a measure of one's love
during lengthy dissertations
to stand unflinchingly at ground zero
is this not the stuff
heroes are made of?

it takes real dedication
to have intimate conversations
with someone whose fierce exhaust
can foul a gymnasium
and to do it in a Volkswagen bug

when we are together
the breeze always comes
from the direction of the dump
"something must be terribly wrong
  with the pump
  at the sanitation plant!"
yet i staunchly remain faithful
after each hug
holding my breath out the door

it takes more
than a little affection
to be friends
with a talking stock yard
to always be there when needed
and at the same time
be up wind

God knows
i've tried to clear the air between us
dropping Dentyne hints

71

or more subtly
calling your attention
to all the creativity it takes
to make an effective Listerine ad
to say nothing about the fortune
squandered on your behalf
carloads of Certs purchased
and sprinkled in your path
placed strategically on car seats
in coat pockets
and all to no avail

it's obvious
i should simply sit you down
and give it to you straight
but when
it comes to finding the nerve
i always find i fail

a poem
an ode to an anonymous friend
is the best that I can do
and if you come away from reading this
unrecognized and unaware
then i guess you'll never know
you have a breath that curdles air

as for me
an ill wind calls my bluff
no matter how much i say i care
i've never cared enough

ANOTHER WAY
OF LOOKING AT IT

until digested
what we put into our stomachs
is still
on the outside of us

male/female
young/old
it matters not

each of us
is simply an object
with a hole through it

stretch the imagination
and people
are really shaped like innertubes
doughnuts and bagels
gentiles and jews

Happy Endings
in the Badlands

HAPPY ENDINGS
IN THE BADLANDS

two over-the-hill actors
still play tug of war
with your mask Kimasabee
not that they need the money
they don't
it's just that they won't
give up the tyranny of the dream—
silver bullets and white hats
are hard to let go of—
i know

there's lots of dust and excitement
surrounding the arrival and departure
of the Wells Fargo Stage—
lots of "yeah!" and "ya-hoo!"

however
out near the sixty-mile marker
at a complete standstill
the question arises
who drives the wagon
when ambition and necessity
no longer work for you?
when the grubstake days are over
and you've settled for something less
than being number one
who cracks the whip
and rides shotgun then?

enter the grinning bandito
enter what looks like the end
with pistol in hand
and instructions
to reach for the skies!

and take it from me
it's not easy
to keep a positive attitude
with your life passing before your eyes
but
what the hell
i said to myself
if this is it i might as well
sit back and enjoy the show
which i did and while doing so
caught sight of a pilgrim
who looked a lot like me
doing what he wanted to do
going where he wanted to go
and making a living at it

or more precisely
being paid for the living he made
i mean
how lucky can you be?
and with that
the buckboard was back up to speed

who drives the wagon
when ambition and necessity
no longer work for you?
try gratitude
then cue the William Tell Overture
the Long Ranger rides again!

A QUIRK OF TIME

drifts
of flushed adolescents
checking out
the ride and concession area...
in those days we eyed each other hotly
and later returned
with children clamped to our legs
squeeling at the size
of the prize pig

this August however
my dear sweet wife
sits in the middle of our bed
weeping because she no longer
wants to go
to the county fair
as much as she used to

and i
at the first sound of a Skil-saw
out planting a screen of trees
between us and the monstrosity
going up on the property
adjoining ours
something i should have anticipated
and taken care of years ago
        fast-growing eucalyptus—
        Monterey pine

i figure fifteen years
before they do the job

        i'll be in my seventies then

POST-ROTATIONAL NESTAGMUS

the phenomenon occurs
when you look away from a moving object
and get the feeling you're traveling
in the opposite direction

with this in mind
know that my late mother
took great pleasure in predicting
that one day
i'd see the conservative light
in the end
i'll have your bleeding heart
she'd say
like the sorcerous queen in Snow White

her basket
overflowing with polished apples
such as
Richard Nixon was an American saint
and oh how she'd cackle
from behind her right wing
when i'd bite

and aside from throwing tantrums
the only recourse i had
was to keep the beard growing
and guarantee
that on election day
she could count on me
to cancel out her vote
it was that kind of child/parent
relationship
that is
until she went off
to the great Republican Party in the sky

80

leaving me
with a small diversified portfolio
hardly a ticket to Easy Street
but enough
for the "down side"
to make me feel queasy
while watching the broad tape run

enough
to recognize the sound of a last laugh
when i hear one

the sleaze-bag
he became in *Missouri Breaks*

OUT TO THE MOVIES

"i would like to have been friends
  with the poet Stevie Smith"
says Billie Barbara

then amending the statement
"i mean
  i would like to have been friends
  with the actress Glenda Jackson
  in the film
  playing the part of Stevie Smith

in my entire life
i have written only one fan letter—
to Marlon Brando
i was thirteen
he never responded
which turned out to be for the best

after seeing the sleaze-bag
he became in *Missouri Breaks*
if Jack Nicholson
hadn't slit his throat
i'd have done it myself
. . . the creep!"

ON THE TRAGIC DEATH
OF MY LITTLE SELF

i was one
who clung grimly to childhood
still playing with toy soldiers
at thirteen

my favorite
a tiny cast-iron pirate
ruled the shelf
thumbs thrust in a wide belt
legs spread defiantly
scuffed and scarred
from a lifetime of adventure
he was my alter ego
and i called him my Little Self

together we lived through
the Seven-Year Slingshot Wars
trials by fire
mud-slides...cave-ins
unscathed we walked away
from countless tree-fort free-falls
diving to the depths
of Mr. Near's lily pond
we stalked the golden killer whale

and once
the Southern Pacific thundered by
as we stood unflinching
between the clamoring rails
yes my Little Self and i
had survived it all

then one fateful day
fastened securely
to a length of twine

i flushed him down the toilet
and while winding him back to safety
the lifeline broke and he was gone
swept away
in one great resounding rush

oh
the irreversible
unfairness of it all! i wept...
rending my clothes...tearing my hair
refusing to open the bathroom door
till my frightened parents
promised to buy me a new recruit
but it was Sunday
the stores were closed tight

and by Monday it was too late
puberty had arrived
and that brazen
invincible spirit of mine
was lost forever
in a maze of subterranean pipe

OBSTETRICS AT THE RIALTO

*(Written after actually being there to witness
the birth of my first granddaughter
Cara Masten Di Girolamo.)*

"pickles and ice cream?" he gulped
swallowing his gum
the movie-goer limp with laughter
at the dimp he'd suddenly become

i cut my eye-teeth
on these celluloid cliches
on Hollywood tough-guys
unraveling
at the first contraction
helplessly stumbling around
fumbling with the car keys—
the inevitable motorcycle cop
out from behind a billboard to stop
the wild reckless ride to the hospital
then suddenly goggle-eyed
hopping back on his machine
shouting "follow me!"

and fathers-to-be
unshaven and forlorn
sweating it out
in the maternity ward hall—
chain smoking nail biters
their misery and discomfort
winked at by nurses who knew after all
that by comparison
men will never know real pain
the birthing scene itself
staged not to offend
and therefore indistinguishable
from all other screened medical events
everyone not directly involved
out in the kitchen boiling water

while the camera focuses discreetly
on the doctor's troubled face
as he bends above the thrashing patient
to deliver a baby
sever a leg
the sequences were interchangeable

and in the end
if the hero wasn't left
in a train station leaning on a cane
he'll be pictured passing out cigars
to the back-slapping crowd
at the observation window
proud papas
making goo-goo noises—
faces pressed against the glass—
a school of goofy goldfish
that never failed
to leave us with a laugh

from start to finish
the birthing process
emasculated by the movie version
and not knowing what else to do
John Q. Public and i
imitated art

MOTHER'S VOICE
AS PART OF THE ESTATE

thank god
it wasn't me she doted on
otherwise i'd have been the one
chosen to inherit Birdy
mother's irksome parrot
that dubious honor was bequeathed
to her youngest son—the pet—
the one who could always get
his way with the queen—
got it in the end—
the talking albatross i mean

the rest of us stifling a grin
as we watched the two of them begin
an ephemeral relationship
that didn't make it through the Fall
but then
i doubt if anyone could live
with the disembodied voice
of a dear departed mom
still calling their name
"Donn!!"
still ruling the roost
cigarette hack and all

my daughter Jerri
the Florence Nightingale
of animal husbandry
was next in line to take the orphan in
and climb the wall—
mother's prattling remains
quickly passed along
to an unsuspecting friend

who out of desperation
took the bird
to see a pet psychiatrist
and the fowl lobotomy that followed
exorcised out every vestige
of mother's zany sense of humor
leaving Birdy
well-behaved but spiritless
enunciating
with the generic inflection
of a network radio nonentity

and now that it's over
i kick myself in the pants
for not seizing the opportunity
to tape-record our family history
while i still had the chance

A STIMULATING, FASCINATING TIME
(Song lyric)

I usually find parties
Such an awful bore.
I put in an appearance
And then slip out the door.
But last night you made the difference
And you're still upon my mind.
Last night I had a stimulating
Fascinating time.

I led you to a corner
And from the very start
I could see you were a person
Who made listening an art.
So I wove my conversation
Into an intricate design
And you never missed a single
Subtle turn of mind.

Your face was ever-changing
Over every word I spoke.
I heard your throaty laughter
After each amusing joke.
You followed my life story,
That sad kaleidoscope.
And you wept upon my poems
So filled with shining hope.

What a stimulating evening
I talked till I was hoarse
And the last to leave the party
Well, it was me of course.
Yes, a most exciting party.
You made me glad I came.
And today I'm only sorry
That I didn't catch your name.

THE PETER PAN SYNDROME

Michael
the jeans no longer fit
i have taken to wearing trousers
this
while you run with a crowd
younger than our children
having food fights

Diet Pepsi and aerobics
belly flat as a plank of walnut
reminding me of a time
when i myself tried to beat the devil
winding up "with an old man's head
on a young man's body"
she laughingly said

and yet here you are
armed with a sympathetic ex-wife
racing a Mercedes
through the smoking ruins
of gutted love affairs
thriving on pain like an adolescent
able to rake the most amazing poetry
from off the floor of this furnace

and Michael
except for the dark howl of your eyes
i am envious of everything
but recently i have lost the desire
to drive around with the top down
or fry on a towel poolside
the dancing fool is no more
i pay for my mistakes with Alka-Seltzer

this evening over dinner
i'll interpret our encounter
for my wife
and like an accomplished jazz musician
improvise around the part
where in the sack later
i will be the one with the headache

however
first thing tomorrow
i plan to visit a medical facility
and buttonhole a doctor
requesting
no...demanding
that he find something wrong with me

OLLIE WILLIFORD

April 23, 1987

my bride came landscaped
with a multifarious forest
of colorful relatives
so i really can't say
her notorious grandmother
registered until
at our wedding reception
she got my full attention
with a big fat french kiss

"i'm your grandma Ollie!
  i've been married at least ten times
  i'm gonna live to be a hundred
  and won't be buried until i die!"

after that
i knew which one Ollie was
and carefully kept some distance
between myself
and that amorous antique
that sexy old sneak
"over the hills and through the woods
to grandmother's house we go"
but look out for that peck on the cheek!

in her sixties then
a bonafide sexagenarian
which i completely dismissed
as just another creaky coquette
rickety tease
another advanced case of hotpants

decades later
watching the *Today Show*
she survives

93

waiting for word from Willard Scott
(i wonder if Willard knows
how many venerable vamps
he keeps alive)

and she is alive!
on the edge of a second century
still with a roving eye
trillium pinned to her blouse
still with her arms reaching out
a living example of never-say-die
the original Granny Goose

and Ollie
while there's still time to tell you
i am seduced

A DAYS OF YORE BORE

i am worried
about the kind of old man
i'm going to be
i fret
because i think i met him
twenty years ago
in Pittsburgh
after a reading of my poetry

clearly his intent
was to simply pay
a fellow-author a compliment
but the moment he had me by the hand
almost helplessly he began
beating his own drum
assaulting me
with unbroken paradiddles
of past accomplishments

and if i hadn't been rude
cutting him off curtly
i suspect
i'd still be in Pittsburgh
wiggling uncomfortably
tangled in the endless resumé
of this aged Lilliputian

but then
looking at it
from his point of view
a compliment doesn't mean much
when you don't know who
it's from

"here
  let me give you one of my books"

in order to have an identity
some of us need
to be preceded by our deeds
ask me who i am
and i'll show you what i do
only recently
coming to realize
that a day may come
when i'm too old to do it anymore
and god forbid
must introduce myself
by telling people what i did

"i don't mean to be a bore
  but..."

if ever
i get you by the ear
and won't let go—read this!
with each passing year
it becomes increasingly
more important for me to know
that you know
that i once knew
what's happening here

REQUIEM
for Sharon Christa McAuliffe

some say that you
and the Challenger crew
came to a tragic end
but when i recount the story
of your star-crossed flight
when i describe the circumstance
surrounding your death
i will do so in the same breath
i used to tell about a comic
who died
at the height of his career
on stage cracking a joke
the laugh still building

and so dear teacher
the tears are not for you
but for an assembly
of cheering students
there to wish you bon voyage
it was Times Square New Year's Eve
until the explosive arrival
of childhood's end
the premature loss of innocence
caught
wearing a birthday-party hat
clutching a tin kazoo
no dear teacher
the tears are not for you

the grief i feel
is for the other finalists
the nine who just missed the boat
one minute wrestling with envy
the next flooded with relief

countervailing emotions
separated only
by a startling puff of smoke
the castaways drenched with guilt
at what they felt
when the call came
and they were granted
that last-minute reprieve
i grieve for them dear teacher
not for you

but most of all i'm angry
at myself for being fascinated
by the telescopic view
of your forlorn family
huddled on the dock
waving goodbye to the Titanic
and angrier still that i would sit
watching grainy pictures
shot from ambush
of small children
getting in and out of limousines
for this rude intrusion
i am truly sorry
but not for you

dear teacher
how can i be anything
but overjoyed
for someone
destined to spend eternity
aboard a great plumed ship
steaming out
across a bay of cobalt blue

you
at the rail
dreaming
forever leaning toward Orion

would that we all could say
on our dying day
that we went out
loved
loving
and on our way

(January 28, 1986)

let it be a dance!

100

THE DANCE BENEDICTION

let it be a dance!
let life be a dance
because we dance to dance
not to go anywhere
and
let it be a danﺍe!
let life be a dance
because within the dance
we move easily with the paradox
knowing
that for every step forward
there will be a step back
and anything else
would have us
marching away from the music

PHOTOGRAPH JERRI HANSEN

Ric Masten and Reed Farrington

About the author:

Ric Masten was born in Carmel, California, in 1929. He has toured extensively over the last 22 years, reading his poetry in more than 400 colleges in North America, Canada and England. He is a well-known conference theme speaker and is a regular on many television and radio talk shows. He lives with his wife Billie Barbara just south of Carmel in the Big Sur mountains.

About the artist:

Reed Farrington was born in 1938 in Parker, Arizona, and was raised and schooled on the Eastern seaboard, graduating from the United States Naval Academy in 1963, and the San Francisco Art Institute in 1970. His early influences were the California figure painters and the American Abstract Expressionists. He lives and paints in Big Sur, California.

103